Poetry Non-stop

Unlock your poetic muse and write a
poem a day for 30 days

Patrick Widdess

Contents

Acknowledgements 1

Introduction...2

Who is this book for?..3

Can I really write 30 poems in 30 days? 3

Who are you and why did you write this book? 4

Writing techniques..6

Get ready! 20

30 poems in 30 days 25

What next? 67

Making your poems shine 71

Conclusion 74

Resources 76

Appendix..79

Acknowledgements

Thanks to everyone who has helped inspire and create this book:

Bridget 'Leggy' Tanner, Ashok Saraf, Ralph Famularo, Robert Lee Brewer, Ruthie Collins, John Mayston and my parents Margaret and Richard Widdess.

Poems in this book were originally published in: Waitrose Weekend, The Guardian, Feeding The Spacemen, Cake, Poems for Peace and Agenda.

Introduction

Welcome to Poetry Non-stop. Every April thousands of poets take up the challenge to write a poem every day for National Poetry Writing Month (NaPoWriMo). Completing the challenge is a huge achievement and a great way to improve your writing. Writing a poem every day for 30 days is an attainable goal for writers of all levels of experience with a bit of commitment and motivation. That said many people fail. It's easy to feel uninspired, get disillusioned with your efforts or get distracted by everything else that happens in your life. The first few times I tried it I gave up after about a week for the reasons mentioned above. This book shares the techniques I used to complete the challenge along with everything you need to remain inspired and motivated throughout the month.

Who is this book for?

Anyone who has an interest in poetry will find inspiration in this book. If you've never written a poem but want to give it a try the prompts, exercises and poems in this book will give you all the inspiration you need. Experienced poets looking for new ideas will gain a boost to their creativity and the material is a valuable resource for creative writing teachers and workshop leaders.

Follow the prompts and exercises in this book and you will soon be writing poems every day that you never thought you had in you.

Can I really write 30 poems in 30 days?

You don't have to be an accomplished poet to complete this challenge. It requires some discipline, motivation and a commitment to silencing your inner critic for a month. If you make the effort to pen a poem every day you will surprise yourself with the results. As you get into the habit it'll become easier and you'll even start to enjoy it.

Even if you don't commit to the challenge you will still find plenty of ideas to spark off new poems along with more than 30 poems I have written in response to the prompts and exercises which I hope you find inspiring and entertaining.
You will find tips on preparing for and completing the challenge later in the book.

Who are you and why did you write this book?

I have been writing poetry since my teens. I took a degree in English literature and creative writing and have since worked as a teacher of English as a Second Language, journalist and copy editor. I grew up in Cambridge and have lived in America, Greece, China, Japan and Poland and currently reside in South Wales. Throughout my varied career I have written poetry. I have been published in *The Guardian; Orbis; Ink, Sweat, and Tears*; *The Liberal*; *Agenda* and other literary websites and publications. I have performed my work internationally and reached the national finals of the prestigious Hammer & Tongue poetry slam several times. I have led creative writing workshops and have always been impressed by the work students produce, even those who doubt their writing abilities. Some of the best work has been by non-native English speakers.

It hasn't been non-stop writing and creativity though. I suffer from laziness and lack of motivation as much as anyone. At times my creativity dwindled to the extent I felt I could no longer claim to be a poet. But I must be a poet because if I go too long without writing something I just don't feel right and then there's nothing for it but to stop procrastinating, get out the notebook and keep writing until inspiration hits, and sooner or later it always does.

Since I was at university I have always got a buzz from instant writing exercises. Being given a prompt and a limited time to produce a piece of writing always gets the creative juices going. I am not always happy with the results, but such exercises have sparked off some of my best poems, and I'm proud to share them in this book.

A few years ago I attended a monthly writing group. The members would take it in turns to produce objects or nominate subjects that we would all spend ten minutes writing about. It built confidence in my ability to write about any topic if pushed to. In 2014 I took the exercise to extremes when I ran a take-away poetry event at an arts festival in Cambridge. I spent the day in a café writing poems on the spot in response to prompts members of the public gave me. It was stepping out of my comfort zone turning the usually private act of writing into a public performance and not only forcing myself to write about any topic I was given but share the results publicly. The experiment worked and I wrote ten poems that day which I was happy with.

Later the same year I completed my first 30 poems in 30 days challenge and produced enough poems I was satisfied with to produce a chapbook called *Feeding the Spacemen*. It was then I decided I had enough experience to write a unique and useful book on the craft of poetry writing. I am confident that whatever your interest and experience of writing you will find pleasure and inspiration within these pages.

Writing techniques

"There's no such thing as writer's block. That was invented by people in California who couldn't write." **Terry Pratchett**

The following chapter introduces a few techniques for generating ideas and poetic forms which can be used to produce quick and satisfying work. There are numerous such forms and techniques. Every poet has their preferred methods and there are many books on the subject. This is a personal selection and you should experiment and familiarise yourself with them all as they will be a vital toolbox when you are writing poems every day.

Brainstorming

You've been given a prompt but you don't know what to write. You've never even thought of writing a poem on that subject. You can't write a poem about that. Yes, you can! And the best way to start writing is to pick up a pen and start writing.

Try this: Pick a noun from a dictionary, newspaper or whatever you can see out of the window. Pick the first thing you come across. Don't be tempted to change it if it seems difficult or uninspiring. Write the word at the top of a page in your notebook. Set your stopwatch for 10 minutes and write everything the word makes you think of. Don't stop to think; don't question, correct or analyse what you're writing. Don't stop writing. Repeat words if necessary and keep going for the full 10 minutes.

When you've finished, look back at what you've written. It may spark off an idea for a poem, but never mind if it doesn't, your brain is buzzing with ideas and material which will provide inspiration in the long run.

This type of exercise should form a regular part of your daily writing routine whether you are writing a poem a day or not. It's the equivalent of a musician practising their instrument every day. The more regularly you write the better you will be.

Pictures

They say a picture is worth a thousand words so if you look at one you'll have plenty to write about. I have a book of hundreds of photos by different artists featuring all manner of different styles and subjects. If I'm stuck for ideas I open it at random for an instant shot of inspiration.

You can use any picture as a source for a brainstorming session. Describe the scene. Ask and answer questions about what you can see. What atmosphere does it convey? What feelings does it evoke? What is the story behind the picture, the people in it and the artist who produced it? What is just outside it? What happened before the moment depicted? What happened after? Can you relate these things to any personal experiences or other stories you have heard? This form of speculation can keep you writing till your hand goes numb.

Pictures can also help when writing to a prompt. If you've done your brainstorm and you haven't come up with any ideas pick a picture and try to link it to the prompt. If there is no clear connection between the two it will push you to think of something really original.

One time I was trying to write a poem on the prompt 'careless'. I selected a random picture of a man in a denim jacket and blue baseball cap sat on a bench. How could that link with careless? I wondered. Maybe he was waiting for someone who had forgotten to turn up. Maybe he'd been left behind… The combination of the picture and prompt quickly led me to write the following poem that I would never have come up with otherwise.

I found the picture on writingexercises.co.uk. Its resources include a page that generates a random photo to use as a writing prompt.

Seeing my son

I saw my son in town today.
He was still sat on the same bench.
I'd quite forgotten telling him to sit and wait
while I spoke with Jenny about their new extension
and the youngest starting school, then
I remembered I'd left my gloves in the bank.
He was always so quiet and patient.
I'd meant to go back and pick him up the next day
but it was my yoga class then a fortnight's holiday.
It must be ten years ago at least and he still has that
Tottenham cap perched, shrunken on top of his head.
As I passed, our eyes met in silent greeting.
I thought of taking a seat next to him
but I couldn't think of anything to say
and he seemed content so I carried on my way.

Research

If you're struggling to get an idea from a prompt, do some research. Suppose your prompt is animals. You are sure to have a favourite animal or one that you found yourself thinking of during earlier exercises. Look it up online, read its Wikipedia page, look at pictures and watch videos. Hopefully you'll discover something surprising or interesting that you can latch onto.

I once had a prompt to write a poem with the title 'It was a _____ and _____ night'. Of course, the famous version of this phrase is 'It was a dark and stormy night'. I did some research into its origin and found it was from the opening sentence of the novel *Paul Clifford* by Edward Bulwer-Lytton. Although the line is often ridiculed I discovered that the author also coined a number of other phrases we use today such as 'the almighty dollar', 'the great unwashed' and 'the pen is mightier than the sword.' I wrote a poem in his defence.

In defence of Edward Bulwer-Lytton

It was a dark and stormy night
was not thought a very bright
way to start an epic work
penned by some pretentious jerk.
Poor Bulwer-Lytton, that one line
saw his name thrown to swine.
It's easy now to forget
that we're all still in his debt.
His hand coined the almighty dollar
and we still adore its power.
It was he who made the unwashed great
Schulz's mocking was an unjust fate.
So heed this genius as you write
and your pen will grow in might.

Acrostics

You have probably come across this form in which each line starts with the letters of the word in the title. It's a form that sets the writer a simple, engaging puzzle.
Write as many words as possible for each letter of your chosen word then use this pool of words to construct your poem.

If nothing else this acts as a more focused brainstorm. Your end result may not be a masterpiece but they are satisfying to put together and may inspire longer works.

Nouns work well especially animals, places and people, though adjectives and abstract concepts can also be interesting to work with.

Feet kick
Ripples across the
Old pond's
Green waters.

At
Last
Only
Nobody
Exists

Haiku

This short and precise form traditionally consists of three lines of five syllables, then seven then five. They are written in the present tense and relate to the seasons.

The rules for modern haiku are a little less rigid but as a general rule they should be three lines describing a single scene, moment or idea. While the syllable count is not rigidly adhered to it is a good idea to try and stick to it initially. It makes you consider the meaning and value of every word which will make all your writing sharper.

Pick an image, a season or a specific memory and brainstorm words and phrases to describe it. Think about the most powerful points of your subject and the words that most concisely describe them. When you have a messy page full of ideas it is satisfying to hone them down until you have conveyed them in three simple, vivid lines.

How pleasant to sit
on the veranda, listening
to the rain falling.

Lying uncovered;
I can still smell my wet hair
even in the dark.

I read today's news
in the paper which lines my
drawer, yellow with age.

Kennings

Kennings come from Viking and Anglo-saxon poetry and are phrases used to describe objects without naming them. They are the poetic equivalent of Instagram – adding an arty filter to any everyday word the form is applied to. Here are some examples of kennings that describe the sea:

Bed of fish, smooth path of ships, island-ring, realm of
lobsters, slopes of the sea-king, whale-house, land of the
ocean-noise, blood of the earth, frothing beer of the
coastline...

Here is the structure of a kenning:

	Base word	Determinant	Referent
battle moon	moon	battle	shield

The referent is the object being described and is not named
directly. The base word stands in for the referent. In this
example the moon is used because it is round like a shield.
The determinant helps us to understand the base word in
terms of the referent. The moon could be a metaphor for
lots of things. In battle moon it must mean shield because
they are used in battles.

Here are some more kennings. See if you can guess what
they are describing, then check the answers at the end of
this section.

1. Life liquid
2. Sky candle
3. Weather of weapons
4. The timber fast boat of the building plot
5. One-eyed picture box

Now try to create a kenning. First pick something to be the
referent – the thing the kenning describes or refers to.

Next write a list of base words – metaphors that look like or represent the word. Try to think outside the box but don't dismiss the obvious. A list for cup might look like this:

Cup

pot
well
pond
lake
crater
vessel
bucket
mouth
socket

Now write a list of determinants – words which are associated with your object in some way.

Cup

drink
liquid
tea
coffee
breakfast
refreshment
morning
teatime
cafe
water
pottery
china
hot

Finally combine a base word and determinant to make kennings. Try a few combinations.

coffee pond
breakfast well
pottery mouth
teatime crater

Finally try to expand some of your best ones into longer phrases:

Sleep-drowning well of the breakfast table.

Who would have thought a humble cup could be so poetic?

You can use kennings in poems to create more original and vivid descriptions as in the following sonnet which includes a couple of examples.

Bison

The village sleeps beneath the pale light
from the silver guardian of the night.
Man's lease upon this land is put on hold
In this hour – silent, still and cold.

Ancient woodland sprawls beneath the stars
from its depths a restless wanderer stirs.
Branches part, he lumbers to the road
eyes sparkle, nose snorts weather of its own.

He stamps across unguarded human borders.
Forest empire's mighty night-clad warrior.
He walks among the silent streets alone
past sound sleepers cradled in their homes.

Villagers find his footprints when they wake
and in fragmented dreams they see his face.

Exercise answers:

1. Blood
2. Sun
3. War
4. House
5. Camera

Limericks

Limericks offer a satisfying challenge of encapsulating an idea within a limited space and a fixed rhyme scheme. They are usually humorous but don't have to be and are a great vehicle for puns, wordplay and irony. They don't have to be about an old man or woman from wherever though those lines offer many possibilities, even more than Edward Lear thought of.

A fun exercise is to take an existing poem or story and rework it into a limerick. The Bible has been rewritten as a series of limericks. Here is a limerick inspired by an episode of the Twilight Zone, *Time Enough At Last*:

A bomb-blast left a bookworm alone
with the time to read tome after tome.
But what a poor bloke!
He foolishly broke
his specs. What a fate to bemoan!

I wrote this for a child who wanted a poem about a vampire:

There once was a vampire called Peter
who was the most fussy young eater.
When served blood every day
he shouted: "No way!
"Just give me a coke and a pizza."

Triolets

The triolet is another short form with a very precise structure. It's a harder form to write but good for structuring an idea into a short poem. The eight line structure follows a set rhyme scheme and the same two lines open and close the poem. The first line is also repeated in the middle. The structure looks like this:

A
B
a
A
a
b
A
B

The capital letters indicate lines which are repeated. The key is finding a strong couplet which can act as a refrain throughout the poem with the other lines adding meaning or detail.

Try writing out the rhyme scheme down the margin of your notebook. Write the opening two lines and fill them in on the appropriate lines. Remember the first line is also repeated on the fourth line. Then try to fit the rest of the lines in. It's tricky to fit all the lines together but the restrictions help you get to the heart of your idea and to express it in an original way.

The following triolet is based on a real-life experience. It was like being caught in a living metaphor but for a long time I didn't know how to write about it. Using the triolet structure helped me translate it from a personal experience to a poem representing, I hope, more universal experiences of love lost and moving on.

Going up

The escalator goes one way   A
as I spot you in the crowd below. B
You smile as I return your wave. c
The escalator goes one way. A
Six weeks ago you went away, a
became someone I didn't know. b
The escalator goes one way A
as I spot you in the crowd below. B

19

Get ready!

"I must write each day without fail, not so much for the success of the work, as in order not to get out of my routine." **Leo Tolstoy**

You have now learnt a selection of writing techniques which can help you quickly generate ideas for poems. You are now ready to write 30 poems in 30 days. The following pages contain a prompt for each day, a poem I wrote from the prompt, and plenty of ideas and encouragement to keep you on track. But before you begin here are some tips:

Decide when to start

If you have tried and familiarised yourself with the forms and techniques described in the previous section you're ready to go. Start tomorrow or next week. If you want to make it easy to count the days or you're doing NaPoWriMo wait till the beginning of the month, but start soon. Mark the date on the calendar and stick with it. If you wait for a 'quiet month' you'll be waiting a long time so just dive in.

Make it public

Tell people you're doing it. Post your poems every day on Facebook or your blog. If people are expecting you to produce a poem every day you won't be able to just quietly give up.
Get friends to do the challenge at the same time. Meet up whenever you can and write together and share your work. Writing needn't be a lonely business.

Think about where and when to write

One of the most common excuses people make for writing is they don't have time. It can be easy to feel that between work, family and other commitments your days are too full for something frivolous like writing poetry but take a closer look at your daily routine. You are sure to find pockets of time that you can spend writing. Lunch breaks, bus journeys, first thing in the morning and last thing at night are just a few of the times when you can fit in some time for your writing and you'll find it soon adds up.

Where and when you write is a personal choice. Some writers work best early in the morning, others at night. Some can't write without complete solitude, others draw inspiration from the hubbub of everyday life around them. Think about how and where you write best and commit to making it part of your daily routine.

If you're not sure what works best try the following: Read the prompt as early in the day as possible and spend at least 15 minutes writing. Just brainstorm at first, writing anything the prompt makes you think about. If you don't come up with a poem during this time don't worry – let the prompt sit at the back of your mind as you go about your day. Later come back and focus on getting your poem written. If you got an idea earlier in the day develop it; if not look back on your notes and try using one of the techniques and forms you have studied to write something.

Be positive about everything you achieve

If you do miss a day don't beat yourself up. Pick up with the next prompt the following day. If you can, go back and complete the prompt you missed but otherwise don't worry. The challenge is not about failing or succeeding. It's about developing your writing and seeing what you can achieve. If you write 30 new poems fantastic but writing 20 or so rough drafts is still a lot more writing than you would have accomplished otherwise. Every time you put pen to paper you are succeeding!

Promise yourself, however, that you'll spend at least 15 minutes writing, even if it's just random brainstorming. It might lead to something and even if it doesn't it will make it easier to write something the next day. If you don't write at all you will lose the momentum that makes this process so effective.

If you can't be original...

As a general rule, cliches should be avoided but when you're writing new material every day it's hard to be original all the time. Don't let yourself get stumped. Write whatever you can to keep the creative flow going.

I think of cliches rather like scaffolding in early drafts. If I can't think of an original way to say something I'll use a cliche just to hold the piece together. Later I can go back and replace it with something stronger and more durable.

Silence your inner critic

Don't worry about the quality of your work. You have enough to do writing the poems without deciding if they are good or not. Just concentrate on writing a poem each day. If you don't like it, you may think of something better later on but if not just put it to one side and get ready for the next day. If you're consistent the writing will get better.

Keep going

Just as it's easy to give up when things aren't going well there's a danger of becoming fixated on a really strong poem. It's tempting to keep working and polishing a poem that you're pleased with or to bask in the glory of your creative genius only to find you've fallen a few days behind. You will also find that a successful day can be followed by one or two difficult ones. Don't worry if a poem isn't as good as the last one you wrote. Just keep going!

However well or badly your poem comes out, once the next day rolls around put it to one side and get working on the next one. You'll have time to work on improving your poems later on: when you come back to them having left them for a week or two you will find it much easier to see their strengths and weaknesses.

Follow your muse

The advantage of writing to prompts is you don't have to feel ashamed of what you write. If you produce something that's terrible, it's not your fault, you didn't choose to write about that. On the other hand when you write something good you claim 100 per cent of the credit! You may find that in trying to write to some of the prompts you are led to write about something completely different. That's a perfectly valid outcome. A poem is a poem. The prompts are designed to ignite your creativity, not restrict it.

Be excited

Your mind is bursting with poetic possibilities. If you stick to the plan you will unleash that creativity and pen poems you never thought you had in you. Those poems are

somewhere in your mind now, waiting to be uncovered.
Get ready for an amazing month of poetry!

"What do you do when you have writer's block?"
"I lower my standards and carry on."
        William Stafford wrote a poem a day for 50 years!

30 poems in 30 days

If you've jumped straight to this section go back and read the earlier chapters. You'll be much better prepared for the following if you do.

Day one: Food

"One cannot think well, love well, sleep well, if one has not dined well." **Virginia Woolf**

Let's kick off with a familiar topic and a menu bulging with possibilities. Think about meals, foods you love, foods you hate, special foods, sweet and savoury, texture and flavour. If you need more inspiration take a stroll round the market or consider the crumbs on your plate after breakfast. Maybe there's a poem in there like tealeaves spelling out your fortune.

When I was trying to think of a food-themed poem for a competition I was reminded of a time I was teaching English to a class of foreign students. The word pineapple came up and several students of different nationalities remarked that it was called ananas in their language. It got me wondering why it had such a strange name in English. I wrote this poem which won second prize.

Pineapple

The pineapple's a funny fruit. It doesn't grow on pines,
And it's clearly not an apple, even if you're blind.
Its skin is thick, inedible and neither red nor green.
It'll cause some grief and break your teeth if bobbed at Hallowe'en.
It grows on the end of a prickly stalk, a most peculiar tree.
If the serpent had offered one to Eve she'd have said: "No, not for me."
It's time to ditch this silly name. It really is bananas!
Let's join the rest of Europe and rechristen it ananas.

Day two: How to...

"No thief, however skilful, can rob one of knowledge, and that is why knowledge is the best and safest treasure to acquire." **L. Frank Baum**, The Lost Princess of Oz

Today write a poem that explains how to do something. Anything from making a cheese sandwich to flying or disappearing has possibilities. Try to be precise and vivid in your instructions. Be imaginative in the steps taken and how you explain them and try to weave some poignance, humour or deeper meaning into your poem.

Look everywhere for inspiration. I was in Japan when I tried this prompt and seeing some octopus displayed in a small restaurant sparked off this:

How to catch an octopus

Familiarise yourself with salt water.
Bathe and brush your teeth with it.
Use it as perfume.
Drink a little at meal times.
Keep an ice cold tank
and submerge your hand for one hour daily.
Do not clench your fist.
Let your hand float free beneath the water.
Over time your fingers will become blubbery
flex the joints so they move with any current.
When you can lift a dinner plate using only your flat palm
find a rock or take a boat out
and wait for your five-legged octopus to find a companion.
Do not grab too soon or resist the draw of the ocean.
Wait till you forget you are waiting
and your hand swims deeper.

Day three: Hometown

"Home is a name, a word, it is a strong one; stronger than magician ever spoke, or spirit ever answered to, in the strongest conjuration." **Charles Dickens**

Write a poem about your hometown – the place you live or where you grew up, a place so familiar you may never have thought of writing about it. Take a walk round your neighbourhood, brainstorm your feelings and memories about the place. Read the local paper, do some research into local history online or at the library and you're sure to uncover some interesting stories and photos. What has changed? What has stayed the same? Think about the people that live here now and in the past.

This is a poem about the road where I was born and grew up near in Cambridge. It was written as part of a sequence of poems about the city performed in collaboration with Cambridge musician Tom Adams.

Mill Road

A scroll unrolled across the fields
decorated and annotated over the centuries.
Those who made the first inscriptions
would scarce believe their land
would turn to city streets, and the dirt track
from town to country become a road
where horseless vehicles hurtle to and fro
and over a bridge where no river flows.
There was a mill when there were fields,
Later a projector whirred where sails once turned,
in a magic picture palace, the world contained in one dark room.
People came in droves to watch cowboys and Indians,

jungles, pyramids, medieval battles and other Hollywood lies
made true in a rapid dance of shadow and light.
Then it was gutted and became a retail revolution.
Checkouts rang out down neon-lit aisles
with shelves stacked high with packets and tins
and refrigerators humming with years' worth
of fish fingers, vegetables and a multitude of ice cream flavours.
The road became an atlas of curry, sushi,
fish and chips, kebabs, noodles, stir fry,
French, Italian, American and Turkish coffee.
Every day shoppers, traders, residents, street poets and alehouse philosophers
work like sails, cogs and pulleys interconnecting
keeping the energy flowing from Petersfield to Romsey
through Arjuna's sunflower fronted vegan emporium,
grocers' rainbow arrays of fruit and veg,
secondhand bookshops with rows of vanilla volumes,
Bakers, beer shops, opticians, tattooists,
Gees electrical museum, Al-Amin's little India,
illuminating trees on cold winter nights,
yarn-bombing the bridge of multi-coloured eyes,
stars, flags, planets and snails.
On it goes through the pharmacist, acupuncturist,
tanning booths like unmarked Tardises,
cycle shops with rows of rusty racers
and brand new bikes with golden frames and wicker baskets,
shops full of everything and nothing in particular,
pubs, restaurants, churches, Hindu shrine and mosque.
The world came to Cambridge and found a home here
The terraced houses and shops are pages in a pop-up encyclopaedia.
The scroll is still illustrated and annotated by those who live here

work here, trade under their own names,
worship their gods, shop and dine here.
The scroll rolls on to future lives and communities
a multicoloured palette, our glowing legacy.

Day four: Back together

"True friends are always together in spirit." **L.M. Montgomery**

Friends reunited or lovers, bands, classmates, relatives and many more. People get back together at many times for many reasons intentionally or by chance. These reunions may turn out well or badly. A broken toy or vase put back together could also unlock powerful feelings and memories.

I wrote this after thinking of all the bands that have reformed recently, with varying degrees of success.

Reunion

They toast their success with champagne,
even teetotaller Mike makes an exception,
then they start to play.
Voices warm, fingers grow supple
as they sing songs that take them back
to arenas, screaming fans
and appearances on Top of the Pops.

Later Dave recalls
how he wrote their first hit
in a Paris hotel
and John says no, he wrote it.
They start to bicker and Mike,
who's had a few more exceptional drinks,
tries to break it up but breaks it open.
The punches fly sharp and strong as the
'Brawl' and 'Bust Up' headlines that follow.

Day five: Mythology

"I liked myths. They weren't adult stories and they weren't children's stories. They were better than that. They just were." **Neil Gaiman**

Every culture has a rich mythology with many weird and wonderful stories and characters. Explore some of these myths to find inspiration for today's poem. You could retell a myth using a poetic form or tell it from a different perspective (Carol Ann Duffy's *The World's Wife* looks at myths and moments in history from a female perspective.) Take a mythological character and put them in a new context. Urban myths as well as a wealth of ancient mythology from around the world could provide inspiration.

For the poem below I focused on an important part of a well known myth about creation which is not usually explained in great detail.

Seizure

Having never done a stroke of work
or had a day of sickness in his life,
he could not fathom the growing pain in his chest,
his ribs tightening around his heart
until the agony drove him to bed and a restless slumber.
Waking later in the grip of a seizure
he put his hand to his heart
and five ribs clothed in fresh skin
took a hold and clasped tight
with crude joints until he passed out.
Running through dark terrain,
tripping over sharp rocks,
his mind tore through nightmares
until a dim light began to grow
and the ground became soft and warm to the touch.
Half sleeping he ran his hand over the limb draped across
his chest
caressed the supple skin over smooth curves
until a sigh aroused him.
Turning to the figure at his side
he met her gaze, and when she kissed him
her lips tasted of sunlight.

Day six: I spy

"A writer, I think, is someone who pays attention to the world." **Susan Sontag**

Today, observe places and people, eavesdrop on conversations. If possible, discreetly follow someone and use your best Sherlock Holmes powers of observation to guess or imagine who they are, what they're doing, what their past, present and future might be… then write a poem about it.

I host a poetry podcast and always ask the poets I interview to provide a prompt for myself and listeners to write a poem for. When I interviewed award-winning poet Jonathan Edwards he gave me two prompts. This was one of them (he uses it very effectively in his collection *My Family and Other Superheroes*). The other was to write a sonnet with a twist. Being ambitious, I combined the two to write this sonnet inspired by a man I observed on a train. You don't have to write a sonnet. Take inspiration from the world around you in whatever form it comes.

Broken chair

He has the stature of a broken chair
burgundy face and a haystack of hair.
His limbs shun symmetry slumped in his seat,
a rubble of bags on the floor by his feet.

He slumbers at last on this homeward train
after cold nights spent alone in the rain
abandoned by mates, made sick on bad pills,
his future spelled out in credit card bills.

But next day he's back in a shirt and tie
bragging to all about how he got high.
Pill popping, parties and multiple lays
make others feel their lives are too grey

makes them feel sad and uniquely alone
mistaking a broken chair for a throne.

Day seven: News

"News travels fast in places where nothing much ever happens." **Charles Bukowski**

Read the newspaper, listen to the radio, go online. There are thousands of stories in the news every day. Some are good, many are bad, a few are touching or funny. Delve into these stories. Think about the people and places involved and write today's poem. Don't just stick to headline news either. There is an abundance of interesting and quirky stories hidden away in local newspapers and the inside pages of the nationals.

This is a limerick based on a story about a guy who got served a hefty wine bill after failing to check the price properly.

A short-sighted man out to dine
chose a 40 quid bottle of wine.
It tasted quite bland
and cost nearly four grand!
Now he keeps his specs on all the time.

Day eight: Animals

"Some people talk to animals. Not many listen though. That's the problem." **A.A. Milne**

If you've been keeping up you've written a poem a day for a week now. Don't worry if you're a bit behind, just keep writing. Today's prompt offers plenty of opportunities. Write about a pet, a favourite animal, an animal that scares you or some bizarre creature on a nature documentary. Think about what different animals symbolise, their place in history, literature and mythology. Write about a single animal or a whole menagerie.

I wrote this while living in a bedsit that was frequently invaded by slugs. No slugs were harmed in the making of this poem.

Slug

I do not hear its single foot
slip beneath my bed,
turn dust into silver
and make a soggy doily
of last month's gas bill.
But the morning sheds light
on its nocturnal wanderings
charted in dry mucus,
its glittering autograph
scrawled across yesterday's paper.
I set mouse traps with lettuce leaves,
surround my bed with half-empty beer glasses,
scatter pellets like deadly confetti.
I sleep well for a week
then find a survivor;
inch long and mossy green,
relaxing by the radiator.
It's then I notice the leafy odour,
and the rug; tacky underfoot.
I dare not look beneath the bed
but lie awake, ear pressed to the mattress.
At dawn I start to drift
and sense the bed being lifted
on a thousand slithering backs,
doors sliding open, and the morning air;
cold and sharp against my cheek.

Day nine: Conflict

"Ideas stand in the corner and laugh while we fight over them." **Marty Rubin**

Think bickering, quarrelling, arguing, fighting, battles and all out war. From Cain and Abel to the world wars conflict has been part of the tapestry of human life and a recurring theme in literature.

This is one of those themes where it's quite easy to churn out doggrel but difficult to write anything original that has an impact. Avoid melodrama. You don't have to write about a major conflict. Your poem could even be funny. Think mismatched couples, absurd arguments and comical misunderstandings.

I was asked to write a poem about war for an anthology. I found it difficult to address the topic as I have been fortunate enough not to have experienced war. I researched accounts of people who have been caught up in conflict and was inspired to write the following about the experiences of a girl in Somalia.

Hands

Her scars are the words her hands can't write,
mangled stumps on a body not yet full grown.

She was searching for her father.
There had been an attack.
Her mother had vanished four months ago
and brother too, lost in the city's torn sinews
where her father might still be alive.

In the aftermath an explosion
shook the neighbourhood and ripped her arms apart.

She would like them to see her,
those who wave from the front pages of the paper.
Those who sign contracts and treaties,
who lay wreaths and salute their troops.
Those whose hands move hands around the world
but didn't lift a finger the night she ended up in this
hospital
where her father may never find her.

Now other hands feed and tend her
but cannot repair the broken skin and shattered bones,
the flesh and blood too widely scattered to restore.

Day 10: The problem with...

"If a problem is fixable, if a situation is such that you can do something about it, then there is no need to worry. If it's not fixable, then there is no help in worrying. There is no benefit in worrying whatsoever." **Dalai Lama XIV**

Take the phrase above and use it to begin your poem. There are many problems large and small, serious and silly. Describe them creatively, offer imaginative solutions and think up unexpected consequences. There are many ways of addressing this problem prompt.

We are often warned about the dangers of rising sea levels. I took a surreal look at what life might be like in such a situation.

The problem with living under water

At least getting out of bed's easy.
You're usually out already, tangled in the duvet,
weighty as a whale's waistcoat, then it's time to dress.
Socks stick to the ends of your feet,
trousers pull you in all directions
shirts billow and won't be buttoned.
No chance of a hot bath,
or invigorating cold shower.
Breakfast is bread that's too soggy for fish food
and cornflakes and milk that don't mix.
The newspaper floats through the letterbox
and disintegrates before you've read the front page.
No time to sit down with the crossword.
No time for anything now the car's broken down
and the walk to work takes four hours.
Why bother when you arrive to a desk full of rusted
stationery,
waterlogged documents,
a malfunctioning PC,
and weak, lukewarm coffee?
And every minute, gasping, you ascend to the surface,
breathe deep and return to this world
where it takes twenty minutes to tie a shoelace
and we speak in a silent language of bubbles.

Day 11: Machines

"A poem is a little machine for remembering itself." **Don Paterson**

We live in a world of machines from smart phones to electric tin openers. Then there are machines of science fiction; starships, teleporters and androids – blurring the lines between man and machine.

Think about machines of the past, present and future. Consider their appearance and functions and how these can be described creatively. I wrote about a machine I use every day, one I know so well it almost feels like a friend.

Bicycle

Hi-yo Silver
sleek metallic beauty
faithful Rocinante.
Murder going uphill
Red Rum coming down.
Hurtling into the wind
I hear Pegasus' wings unfold.

Day 12: Not what it seems

"The more I see, the less I know for sure." **John Lennon**

Write a poem in which something is not what it seems; an elderly newsagent who's a top international spy, a rusty gate that leads to another world, a devoted husband or wife with a dark secret. Try taking a walk and use your imagination to invent new stories and meanings for the people and places you see.

I wrote the poem below after passing a decrepit roadside memorial and wondering what it was commemorating.

Memorial

Twelve months on and withered bouquets
are held together by blackened ribbon
untouched by street cleaners out of respect
plastic wrapping entwined in the fence.
A couple of teddy bears sit eyeless
and ruffled by snow, rain and exhaust fumes,
soggy bellies bulging with maggots and bacteria.
What are they doing here?
There are many answers.
A two-year-old victim of a hit-and-run,
a student mown down on her bicycle,
that teenager stabbed by a gang.
All and none of these are true.
A couple driving to a lunch do
on the hottest day of the year
found their gift wilting bloom by bloom
until they left it by the road side
before stopping at a store for fresh supplies.

Day 13: Blind

"There is a condition worse than blindness, and that is, seeing something that isn't there." **Thomas Hardy**

Blind as a bat, love is blind, three blind mice, blind man's buff. Blind is a word that comes up in all manner of contexts. A world without sight can be a very strange and alien place but one can also be blind through being ignorant or stubborn.

My poem was inspired by a time I took a group of students to London. One girl lost her camera and it made me think about how we can become blind through not being observant and failing to live in the moment. Don't be blind to the possibilities of this prompt.

Mementos

She tries to recall the soldiers' uniforms, how they marched and the size of the horses.
Buckingham Palace and the front of the British Museum blur in her mind.
All she remembers of Trafalgar Square is other tourists, a selfie with a lion and quick glance at Nelson.
She tries to piece together all the sights, scenes and moments she never really saw or lived as she snapped them for posterity on the camera, swallowed forever in the subterranean sprawl of the Tube.

Day 14: Repetition

"It's the repetition of affirmations that leads to belief. And once that belief becomes a deep conviction, things begin to happen." **Muhammad Ali**

You are now two weeks into the challenge and the writing process may be feeling a bit repetitive so use some repetition in today's poem.

Repetition is great for emphasis and building strong rhythms. You can repeat words, lines or a repeated rhyme scheme. You could also write about something that happens repeatedly, or something that might happen again or that you want to happen again. Anyway you get the idea. I don't want to keep repeating myself.

Never again

Remember, remember and never again
the fighting, the killing, the loss of young lives.
We solemnly vow to allow peace to reign.
Remember, remember and never again.
But they say we must fight for the peace to remain
and the soldiers march on until once more we cry:
remember, remember and never again
the fighting, the killing, the loss of young lives.

Day 15: Famous

"Fame means millions of people have the wrong idea of who you are." **Erica Jong**

After today's poem you will be half way through. Well done and keep it up!

Today, write a poem about or inspired by somebody famous. Flick through the newspaper, the pages of Hello! and see if you can turn a bit of celebrity gossip into a poem. Alternatively, you could write a homage to your favourite singer, movie star or even poet. Write about someone currently in the public eye or a historical figure. Look up interesting facts about your chosen subject or use your imagination to parody them or put them in an unusual situation.

Here's a poem about how one scientist's most famous discovery could have made him a bit of a spoilsport.

Newton

We used to be free, lightly treading over treetops,
making sport on flying brooms,
turning somersaults over the moon.
Then Newton taught us
about the force that binds us,
laid down laws dictating that we cannot and will not leave the ground.
We still do of course, when he's not around,
dropping to our places when he enters the room.
The braver pupils hover an inch above their chairs,
dare each other to float to the ceiling
when he turns his back to write on the board.

Day 16: Surrender

"At fifteen life had taught me undeniably that surrender, in its place, was as honorable as resistance, especially if one had no choice." **Maya Angelou**

Surrender your heart, surrender goods, surrender to the enemy. Surrender to the possibilities of this prompt but resist the temptation to give up.

This poem shows the benefit of getting out in the open air for inspiration. I had been trying to come up with an idea for this prompt for some time when I went out for a walk in the park. It was late autumn and when I got back, my mind was buzzing with this:

Autumn

I walk among the blazing trees showering golden embers
My steamy breath shouts silent wows at summer's bold surrender.

Day 17: Release

"Captivity ends when creativity begins" **Constance Chuks Friday**

There are many ways to go with this prompt. You can be released from a prison or a contract. Animals are released into the wild. There are many ways to release pressure and emotions. Plants release seeds into the wind. Escapologists have to release themselves. Products are also released – often with far too much hype.

New release

We have been here since before sunset and the early morning light is as sickly as our sleep deprived bodies. We stand to attention as the store lights come on. Fatigue evaporates as the staff come to the door. Then they unleash the storm. We charge. Some push ahead, others pull us back. An old man falls and paramedics attend. We pass the doors and battle the surge driving us into sharp-edged tables and heavy shelves, then we're herded into line. With nowhere to go we catch our breath, agonise at the sight of the dwindling pile of stock as customers proceed to the counter. Time slows. Time slows, until we can count those before us. It drops to ten then five. Three... two... one, and we head to the counter.
Before we know it we're walking away giddy and ecstatic. I look in disbelief at the bright white box in my hand. The very latest paper clip. Such a beautiful shape.

Day 18: Mundane

"Creativity is piercing the mundane to find the marvellous." **Bill Moyers**

Writing a poem every day is not easy. You have to be ready to take inspiration from anywhere. Today write a poem about something mundane: washing up, getting dressed, brushing your teeth... Try to find metaphors in these activities, link them with other aspects of life and the world or find original ways of describing them. I was given this prompt when I did a podcast with Christina Thatcher who often draws on mundane matters when writing about heavy topics like love, life and death. I used kennings as a starting point. Remember how I said they could add an arty filter to any everyday word? I came up with the kenning face antlers for facial hair and that was the starting point for this poem about shaving.

Antlers

I wake, my face bristling with tiny antlers,
twisting into coarse cutlasses and jagged spears,
lined up like troops itching for battle.
But thrusting one's chin at a cashier is no way to rob a bank
and rubbing your cheek in another man's face
will not win an argument or disarm a mugger.
Beard wrestling is yet to be recognised as an official sport.
Afraid of losing myself in this hairy onslaught
I bathe and lather my newly sprouted horns so they stand to attention
then sever them with one clean stroke.
No hunter would mount these meagre trophies on their walls.
They fall and cling to the porcelain against the plughole's soapy gurgle.

Day 19: Small

"Be faithful in small things because it is in them that your strength lies." **Mother Teresa**

For today's poem think small. There are invisible worlds of microbes and amoebas around us. Explore them. Think about how the world looks when viewed by a mouse, puppy or small child or contemplate the power of small things like bullets, deadly viruses and seeds that become huge trees.

Anything can be small depending on your perspective. Planet Earth is one tiny speck in our galaxy which itself is only one of billions of specks of light in the universe.

A grain of sand

Take a closer look at this world,
not uniform yellow but deep maroon
mingled with charcoal grey.
A translucent glassy vein marks the equator.
Across the plains names are etched
in the mystic runes of this land's ancient tongue.
There are mountains, caves and valleys,
roads wind from north to south.
It is dry on all its unmarked continents
until a monsoon comes in a single rain drop
turning the land a darker hue
illuminating scores of jewels embedded in its crust.
The plains are flooded,
mountaintops are islands,
rivers flow through the valleys.
Waterfalls cascade over clifftops
transforming the thinnest threads of sunlight into rainbows.

Day 20: Super hero or heroine

"A hero stands up to the villain in themselves." **Ricky Maye**

The world of superheroes is full of magic, action, adventure and good versus evil. Write an ode to one of these characters, put them in a new context or tell their story from a different angle. You could also create your own super hero or imagine life with special powers. Don't restrict yourself to Marvel comics and action movies. There are many characters throughout literature and mythology who could be considered superheroes with a range of back stories, motives and super powers.

When I tackled this prompt I found myself thinking of Robin Hood but had no idea what to write about. Later in the day I got an email about Sherwood Forest being under threat from destruction and this poem more or less wrote itself.

Robin Hood

I could easily have been real
with the whole of Sherwood Forest to hide in.
And I was real in the hearts of many then and now.

I am all who made a stand,
gave a helping hand,
turned to crime
when the law was an unjust shackle.

Now the world is rigged with cameras,
trees replaced with concrete,
hedgerows with barbed wire.
They may take Sherwood soon,
plough through till every tree
is gone and then you'll know
I'm absent, not just hidden.

Day 21: Time

"Let us never know what old age is. Let us know the happiness time brings, not count the years." **Ausonius**

Write a poem about time. Good times, bad times, night or daytime. The ancient past or the distant future. There's no time like the present to write a poem. Write about how time changes things or what it hasn't changed. You could even write about time travel.

The idea for the following poem came from hearing that the harsh conditions on the moon have caused the flags left by American astronauts to lose their colour, but they remain there still and will do for a long time to come.

Lunar Debris

No Ozymandias ruled this land
where crooked posts like gibbets stand
displaying grey and tattered rags,
remains of long lost nations' flags.
Where did they go? What was the goal
of those heavy-footed souls
whose small and aimless steps remain
cast on this barren, windless plain?

Day 22: Sound

"If music be the food of love, play on…" **William Shakespeare, Twelfth Night**

Open your ears and sounds you have never heard or noticed properly will rain down from all around: birdsong, car radios, overheard conversation, the muffled noises from neighbouring flats, wind and rain. Reflect on these sounds and any others you can seek out or recall as inspiration. You could write an onomatopoeia poem imitating a sound or sounds in a place. Sounds may evoke a scene or memory or you might write about a person's voice or the noise a bird or animal makes.

This is a poem I wrote while I was living in China about a group of traditional Chinese musicians I often heard playing in one of the public squares in the city of Dalian.

The musicians of Zhongshan Square

In a corner of the circle
known as Zhongshan Square
musicians gather each evening.
Concealed by a crowd
they play intently
as if enjoyment is forbidden
oblivious to the onlookers
and the moon drawing near
glowing warm and bright
like the erhu's string
resonating with its tuneful song.
No matter now that the words are foreign,
they speak volumes now they have melody.
Unified the crowd moves closer
as the evening fades
sharpening the blossom notes
drifting from between the players' fingers
and their strong lips
moulding each one with a kiss.

Day 23: Fear

"I'm not afraid of death; I just don't want to be there when it happens." **Woody Allen**

Write about what scares you. Your irrational fears, your darkest nightmares, horror stories on the news or in fiction. Write about overcoming fear or how it can destroy you but don't be afraid of this challenge.

This poem was inspired by a dream I had a few nights before I was given the prompt.

Bite

Six roses sprang from my leg
and melted into mournful rivers
until I sealed them.

For a week phantom teeth gripped my thigh
and wiry grass seemed to grow beneath my cotton skin.

Yesterday six crimson spots like freshly filled wells
were revealed wincing in the light.
Six hearts throbbed beneath scabby mounds
on a pale band of skin.

This morning,
pulling back the covers,
found my knee cap wrapped in roots
and a green stem sprouting from my thigh,
two leaves reaching like a baby's hands,
ripe and pristine.

Day 24: Island

"No man is an island, entire of itself; every man is a piece of the continent." **John Donne**

Islands are places of refuge and isolation. They are miniature worlds full of unknown dangers and possibilities. They give us space to find our true selves and are places of dreams and nightmares.

See where your muse takes you as you conjure up islands real and imagined in your mind.

The following poem was inspired by Sully Island in South Wales. It is a tidal island meaning it can be reached on foot at low tide.

The Island

You can walk there and back at low tide
along the causeway too firm and dry to be the seabed.
But should you cross on the amber light
the sea may creep up from behind
climb wave upon wave
until the path is cut like a taut thread
leaving you drowned or stranded at best.
Fear not, the island offers ample shelter and sustenance.
You may find yourself amongst other refugees
who share their pot of stew and their stories
until you feel the need to loosen your shirt
then discard it altogether as you join them,
rushing to duck beneath the searchlight beam
of the rescue boat as it passes.

Day 25: Backwards

"Life can only be understood backwards; but it must be lived forwards." **Søren Kierkegaard**

Sometimes in poetry it helps to take a new perspective so write a backwards poem. You could write about travelling backwards, time going backwards or doing an everyday activity in reverse. You could write a poem backwards starting from the last line and moving back to the first.

Here's a poem which imagines life going backwards.

How We Forget

Seeing my son born I realised how much I'd already lost.
The cord wasn't even cut before he got to his feet
extended his hand and inquired whether I was his father.
Then he was off explaining quantum physics to the teenage
midwife.
How quickly my days as a CEO passed
and I find myself older than judges and most politicians.
Teenagers are accountants and lawyers,
Prepubescent kids are professors and surgeons
and the prime minister is rarely over forty.
Already my son says he struggles to keep track of the
global economy.
Aged ten his chances of being governor of the bank of
England are already slipping away.
Too soon I've sunk to managing a small branch office
with no better prospects than joining the grey-haired,
balding clerks
before being retired and sent to school where they make
you relearn
all you've forgotten about maths, history and science,
re-teach everything you never have and never will need to
know.
My mother thinks she's in love.
She's long forgotten her forty year marriage.
Now she's obsessed with some guy she met at an over 60s
coffee morning.
She thinks she remembers what love is.
My father has just started crawling.
It won't be long before he says his last words
and is confined to a home
where folk spend their days in bed
sleeping, crying and babbling,
blissfully unaware that they're old and dying.

Day 26: Inevitable

"You can cut all the flowers but you cannot keep Spring from coming." **Pablo Neruda**

Death, taxes, heartbreak, growing old, happy endings in cheesy Hollywood blockbusters are all inevitable. Explore these situations and others where you just know the outcome. It's inevitable you'll come up with a good poem.

This poem was inspired by Angela, a character in the Mike Leigh play Abigail's Party, who inevitably said completely the wrong thing.

Gossip

Stella holds forth at the party
to her husband's silent approval.
She's sworn to secrecy over the news of his promotion.
He offers her more wine and she thanks him,
the pendant on her tight necklace
wagging at her throat like a second tongue.

Day 27: I'll be...

"When I discover who I am, I'll be free." **Ralph Ellison**

Complete this phrase and use it as the title of your poem.
I'll be back, I'll be glad when this is over, I'll be waiting
for you... are a few possibilities. List as many titles as you
can think of and see what sparks your imagination.

I'll be writing in the café

I can just picture you:
Sat at a table with one leg shorter than the other three,
notebook open, well-worn book set nearby like a side dish,
and half empty cup of coffee.
When you look up you have a far off expression.
You put your head down and ink up
page after page with a dense word mulch.
There is also a cigarette smouldering in an ashtray
even though I know you don't smoke and it's forbidden
anyway,
it just fits the picture.

Day 28: Love

"I'm selfish, impatient and a little insecure. I make mistakes, I am out of control and at times hard to handle. But if you can't handle me at my worst, then you sure as hell don't deserve me at my best." **Marilyn Monroe**

You're almost done and if you haven't written a love poem yet it's time to try. Love is all around in our own lives and everyone else's. It's found in nature, movies, literature and art. With so many ways to go this prompt should be easy but of course it's been written about a great deal already. How do you escape the cliches and write something original and meaningful? Think about your own personal experiences, look at a classic love story from a different angle or tell it in a poetic form. And remember this project is about writing every day, not writing something brilliantly original all the time. A 'roses are red…' type verse or two is better than nothing.

Love's organ

Not the heart,
asymmetrical lump of gristle,
but the lungs
intricately crafted bellows
to your flaming soul.
Steadily heaving, infusing
blood with scarlet passion,
feeding air through the throat's fragile machinery
voicing every word, sigh and song.
Bagpipes of Cupid, play on.

Day 29: Direction

"It is because Humanity has never known where it was going that it has been able to find its way." **Oscar Wilde**

Pick a point of the compass and use that to direct your writing. Head up north, fly south, look to the east, head north by north west or some other direction in your imagination.

I tried this prompt when the First World War centenary was being celebrated which took the poem in a harrowing direction.

Deserter

He was heading north having lost his bearings
which was no defence to the generals who had lost theirs.

Day 30: Milestones

"Life isn't a matter of milestones, but of moments." **Rose Kennedy**

Hurrah! The final day of the challenge. If you've kept up you will have 30 new poems after today's prompt. There are many milestones in life from wedding anniversaries to pints of blood given to actual miles run in marathons. These milestones can be marked in many ways. Write about them to reach the 30 poems in 30 days milestone.

Milestones

After ten years they gave me a milestone
which bent my back and sloped my shoulders
until my twentieth year when they gave me a second
which at least balanced the load.
Then they started coming thick and fast:
500 miles walked between my desk and the photocopier,
20,000 cups of tea served,
6 months sat in traffic,
40 years since I last did a cartwheel.
I am one of those men you see in loose suits
cut from the cloth of faded office furniture,
pockets, sleeves and trouser legs bulging with stones.
When I head for the door a trainee opens it for me.
Later the manager hands him a flat pebble.
He tosses it in the air with a flick of the wrist,
puts it in his pocket and continues with a jaunty stride.

What next?

The following section is mainly aimed at beginners and those without much experience of editing and redrafting poems. More experienced poets will have developed their own methods but might find some of the following techniques useful.

Congratulations! Writing a poem a day for 30 days is not easy to achieve but you did it. You may have stumbled along the way and written some verses you are less than proud of but I can guarantee you are a better poet than you were when you started and things are only going to improve.
So far you have just been working on getting ideas down but now you are not writing new poems every day you have time to really make that material shine. There may be poems you think aren't up to much but you may find there are phrases or ideas there which can be developed or used in other works. Hopefully there will be some poems you are really pleased with but they too could do with a polish. But first of all take a rest for a few days. You have been immersed in the writing process for a month and the only way to get the best out of the writing you have produced is to distance yourself from it. Read a book, watch a movie, go out and get some exercise. After you've got the last month out of your system prepare to start editing.

Give yourself a new goal

When you first wrote your poems you had a goal to write a poem every day. Now you need a new goal to keep you motivated and get the best out of your work. When I first completed this challenge, I set myself the goal of producing a 20-page booklet. This gives you a fantastic end product for your efforts. You also have a book you can share with family and friends and sell at readings, local bookshops and online. It will raise your profile as a poet and the fact you wrote the poems in one month will impress readers and create a strong selling point. Alternatively you might want to target poetry magazines or competitions. There is a list of online resources at the back for finding competitions and publishing opportunities. When you are setting your goal, aim for something that will push you to get the best out of your writing, but don't make it overwhelming. Half a dozen magazine or competition submissions is a good amount to aim for.

Having a goal will also give you a focus for your work. If you are producing a book, think about the sort of person who will enjoy reading your poems. Think about their age, appearance and character. What interests do they have? Keep this person in mind as you develop your work. Magazines all have a specific style of writing they publish. Read the submission guidelines and a copy of the magazine. When you work on your poems try to imagine them on the page and ask yourself honestly if they fit in. For competitions look at who is judging them and read their work. Look for any interviews they have given in which they discuss what makes a good poem. Competitions with a theme are good because you have a better idea if your poem fits what they are looking for.

It's also a good idea to find out if there are any open mic nights in your area. These are great events to go to because you get an immediate reaction to your work and have the chance to hear a wide range of other poets and to network with them. If you go regularly you will get to know the core audience well. It's easier to write for an audience you know personally.

It takes some guts to get up and read your work the first time but it really is worth it. Poetry audiences are extremely friendly and supportive. It's not like comedy clubs where new-comers are mercilessly heckled and booed off stage!

Review your work

The following section is not a comprehensive guide to writing and editing poetry, if such a thing exists. There are many techniques and approaches to the craft of writing poetry, enough to fill any number of books. Much of it comes down to experience of writing and editing your own poetry and reading other people's so you gain a stronger sense for what works. The following steps are intended to offer a good starting-point for developing your work, especially if you are new to writing poetry.

Now you've had a rest and got a goal you should be all fired up and ready to read and revise your poems. Go back and read them. Avoid the temptation to start editing them just yet. Give each one your full attention in turn. There will be some lines and even whole poems you have forgotten about in the rush of writing daily.

As you read each poem try to identify the main idea or meaning of each one. You are likely to find that poems you didn't think were any good contain an interesting idea which you can work with. With the poems you consider more successful it helps to think about why they work so you can make them as strong as possible and use similar ideas to write further poems. Try to sum up these ideas in a sentence and write it beneath each poem.

Here are the ideas behind some of my poems:

Broken chair: A man who is sad, lonely and broke convinces others his life is great – a warning against comparing ourselves to others.

Pineapple: A humorous look at why pineapple is a silly and inappropriate name.

How we forget: A world in which everyone starts off very wise and knowledgeable then slowly becomes more foolish and immature as they get older.

Next give each poem a rating out of five. This will make you really think about what strengths and weaknesses each poem has. You will also realise there is a lot more merit in your work than you originally thought.

Making your poems shine

You can now begin developing the poems you feel have most potential. Before, I told you not to worry about the quality of your writing and just get ideas down. Now you must be a harsh critic to make sure that every line, every word is as strong as possible. Most of your poems will be quite rough around the edges but some may already seem complete. The quality of the ideas and wording of these poems can blind you to their weak points. Whatever you think of the poem in its current form you must scrutinise it thoroughly. You may only change one or two words in the end but you will only achieve the best results through a rigorous process of redrafting.

You should address each of the following steps when redrafting your poem. At each stage you may want to make substantial changes, on the other hand you may make just a few small ones, or none at all. If you come to the end of the process and you haven't made any changes be wary: poems sometimes come out perfectly formed, but it's rare. Put the poem to one side for a few days then come back to it and see if it still stands up to scrutiny.

First, make a copy of the poem you are working on so you still have the original version after you've made changes. If you make a number of substantial redrafts keep a copy of each one. It can be interesting to see how your poems develop and you might want to reinstate words or lines from earlier drafts.

Read your poem out loud. It may feel uncomfortable but it's the only way to feel the rhythm and flow of your poem. As you read you will pick up on awkward lines and unnecessary phrases. It also helps with spotting typos as you are reading each word individually rather than skimming over words.

Look back at the sentence you wrote about the idea you are trying to convey. Does the poem convey the concept clearly? Look at each line. How does it contribute to the overall poem? If it doesn't seem to add anything try rewriting it, or get rid of it. You may find there are gaps in your draft that need filling in but you should not be afraid to cut. In poetry less is more. I was once asked to write a poem about the Norfolk Coast. After rambling for line after line about sandy beaches, boats bobbing on the waves and sea breezes I ended up condensing the image I wanted to convey into a two-line poem with none of the bland, predictable phrases above.

Norfolk coast
A salty smile on the breeze.
Beaches stretch from spring to winter.

Think about form. If you've written your poem in a form is it working effectively? Does the language seem forced to fit the form? If so redraft it or try a different form. The form should fit the words, not the other way round. On the other hand, if you've written in free verse your may find you are rambling or finding it hard to structure your poem. Rewriting it in a set form will give it focus and structure.

Think about your use of language. Does your poem convey vivid images and evoke emotions. Are the adjectives, similes and metaphors as strong and original as they can be? Try out alternative versions until you find one that hits the spot. This is not an easy step and only comes from experience. At this point it may be time to get help from outside.

Get some feedback. You still might not be sure if your poem is working. You may be getting frustrated over some part you can't get just right or you may feel that a poem is a work of genius one day and absolutely terrible the next. It can be daunting to share your work but if you don't share it sometime what's the point of writing it?

Start with a sympathetic audience: friends, family or a writing group. Avoid the temptation to explain the poem beforehand or be self-critical of it, just explain that it's a poem you are working on and ask what they think.

People's initial comments tend to be overly positive and non-specific, especially if your critic is not a poet. You need to ask questions carefully to elicit more useful feedback. Ask what they liked about it, ask what they would improve and crucially ask what they think it's about. This will tell you if you have successfully conveyed the idea you were aiming for. If they don't give the answer you were expecting don't correct them, ask them why they think that. It will give an important insight into how other people are interpreting your work. It can be frustrating when people don't understand your ideas but remember, when your poem is out in the wide world you won't be able to go round explaining it to people, and you shouldn't have to.

You don't have to agree with all the feedback you get. Your reader's ideas are not necessarily better than yours but you should certainly consider them. Try changing the poem in response to their feedback and see how it works. You can always change it back again. If you get feedback you are not sure you agree with ask someone else and see if they say the same thing.

To give an idea of this process in practice, there is an explanation of how I developed one of the poems in this book in the appendix. It may seem like a lot of work but you will enjoy seeing your poems take shape and really sparkle. The more you write, the easier it will become to refine your work and produce poems which you will be proud to share with friends and the wider public and excited to get published. So start compiling that book and send off those magazine and competition submissions and good luck!

Conclusion

If you've made it this far you will have some terrific poems which you can now work on getting published. Be proud of yourself; whether you wrote one poem you are pleased with or 30, you now have the skills to keep the inspiration coming and write more and more poems.

Remember to read poetry every day. Keep a note of poems that you like and what impressed you about them. Try to think about what the poet wanted to say and how they managed it so successfully. Listen to poetry on the radio, online or best of all live. Poetry takes on a whole new dimension when it's spoken out loud.

Feed these experiences into your own poetry by continuing to write regularly. Try to write a poem at least once a week. Decide what you're going to write about. It could be something you choose or if you don't have any ideas pick a prompt. There are plenty of places online to find prompts like the ones in this book. There are a few listed in the next section. Once you have decided on a topic or prompt, write it at the top of the page. In this way you are committing yourself and it gets you started with writing. And then remember, whatever your subject, there is a poem out there; you just need to concentrate a while to find it.

Thank you for reading this book. I hope you have enjoyed it and gained something from it. I would love to read the poems you've written and hear about your successes. Please leave me a review on Amazon or contact me using the details below. Thank you once again and happy writing!

Patrick Widdess
2016

www.patrickwiddess.co.uk
info@patrickwiddess.co.uk
Facebook: www.facebook.com/patrickwiddesswriter
Twitter: @patrickwiddess

Resources

Online resources

NaPoWriMo (www.napowrimo.net) – The headquarters of National Poetry Writing Month with prompts and other resources.

The Poetry Foundation (www.poetryfoundation.org) – Poems, blogs, podcasts… a wealth of inspiration.

The Poetry Society (poetrysociety.org.uk) – Useful resources and information on publications and competitions. Membership is a must for anyone interested in poetry.

Poetic asides (www.writersdigest.com/editor-blogs/poetic-asides) – Weekly poetry prompts, daily prompts for NaPoWriMo and other articles and discussions.

Write out loud (writeoutloud.net) – News, features, information on publication opportunities and competitions and a gig guide.

Winning Writers (winningwriters.com) – The best free to enter competitions with an email list to keep you up to date.

Calls for Submissions (Poetry, Fiction, Art) (facebook.com/groups/35517751475/?fref=ts) – A useful Facebook group for hearing about competitions and submission opportunities.

Writing exercises (writingexercises.co.uk) – Various prompts and resources including a random picture generator.

Writers and artists (www.writersandartists.co.uk) –
Resources for professional writing.

Tedx talk by Nicoletta Demetriou
(youtu.be/aTgPJQ9Dy7Q) – This inspiring talk should give
you any extra motivation you need to make writing a part
of your daily routine.

Books

The Poet's Companion: A Guide to the Pleasures of Writing
Poetry – Kim Addonizio and Dorianne Laux

52: Write a poem a week. Start now. Keep going – Jo Bell
– An inspiring book to continue writing poetry on a regular
basis.

Six Poets: Hardy to Larkin: An Anthology – Alan Bennett
– More than just an anthology as Bennett's commentary
helps build a deeper appreciation for the poets and their
work.

The ode less travelled – Stephen Fry – Advice and
exercises for writing poetry.

Poetry Notebook: 2006-2014 – Clive James – A fantastic
poet whose commentaries on poems from Shakespeare to
Larkin and Keats to Pound are well worth reading.

How to be Well-versed in Poetry – E. O. Parrott – A guide
to poetic forms and styles with entertaining examples.

Poetry writing: The expert guide – Fiona Sampson

Podcasts

The New Yorker Poetry Podcast
(www.newyorker.com/books/page-turner/introducing-the-new-yorkers-poetry-podcast)

Headstand (headstandradio.blogspot.co.uk)

The Scottish Poetry Library
(www.scottishpoetrylibrary.org.uk/connect/podcast)

Poetry Foundation
(www.poetryfoundation.org/features/audio?show=The Poetry Magazine Podcast)

Stand Up Tragedy (www.standuptragedy.co.uk)

Appendix

Bison

I was inspired to write this poem about an experience I had when visiting Białowieża, an ancient forest in Poland. A tour guide pointed out some bison tracks on a grassy verge next the road my hotel was on. The thought of a mighty bison wandering the streets, just yards from where I was sleeping, transcending boundaries between man and nature was very evocative but it was difficult at first to shape it into a poem.

This was my first attempt:

He lumbers like a coal heap
in the early, early morning,
when there are no eyes to see him as he strolls.
His eyes shine like two black stars
from his hide of moonless midnight.
He doesn't see the woodland, village, park and fields
only land on which to roam.
He clambers down the bank
to where the path becomes a road;
continues silent as the houses
that stand on either side.
He swaggers down the high street
like a hefty postman,
breathes a final dream
into each sleeping head he passes.
He is gone before they wake
but rough tracks remain on the roadside
to remind them that he's near.

There are a number of lines I like in this draft: 'lumbers like a coal heap', 'hide of moonless midnight', 'swaggers down the high street / like a hefty postman', but it feels rather cluttered and disorganised. When reading it aloud it stops and starts and has no flow. There are also many weak lines that don't say much or say it in an interesting way 'early, early morning', 'silent as the houses that stand on either side'.

Later I tried writing a sonnet, the one earlier in this book. I did not cover sonnets in the section of techniques as they can be quite laborious to write when you're trying to keep up with writing a poem a day but it is a good form to give a poem focus and structure. I also devised kennings to describe the bison and the moon to create tight but original descriptions.

The village sleeps beneath the pale light
from the silver guardian of the night.
Man's lease upon this land is put on hold
In this hour – silent, still and cold.

Ancient woodland sprawls beneath the stars
from its depths a restless wanderer stirs.
Branches part, he lumbers to the road
eyes sparkle, nose snorts weather of its own.

He stamps across unguarded human borders.
Forest empire's mighty night-clad warrior.
He walks among the silent streets alone
past sound sleepers cradled in their homes.

Villagers find his footprints when they wake
and in fragmented dreams they see his face.

I've had to sacrifice the lines I liked in the first draft but this version flows better and has a much clearer structure. I have four lines to set the scene, another four to describe the appearance of the bison, four more for its journey through the village, then just two lines to finish it off.

In the first draft I was free to just throw in line after descriptive line, which is no bad thing at the start but writing the sonnet made me choose my words carefully and the structure helps keep the reader engaged, carries them through the poem conveying an image vividly and succinctly.

Every poem develops differently and the changes can be big or small. I hope these two versions give some idea of the process and how the techniques I've described can help develop and sharpen a rough draft or a poem that's not quite working. Good luck with your writing!

Printed in Great Britain
by Amazon